Anchor Hocking
DECORATED PITCHER AND C

The Depression Years

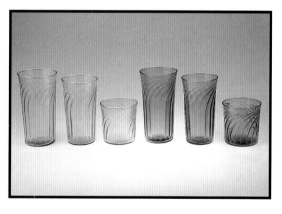

PHILIP L. HOPPER

Schiffer Publishing Ltd

4880 Lower Valley Road, Atglen, PA 19310 USA

Designed by Bonnie M. Hensley
Cover design by Bruce M. Waters
Type set in Americana XBd BT/Zapf Humanist 601 BT

ISBN: 0-7643-1486-6
Printed in China
1 2 3 4

Published by Schiffer Publishing Ltd.
4880 Lower Valley Road
Atglen, PA 19310
Phone: (610) 593-1777; Fax: (610) 593-2002
E-mail: Schifferbk@aol.com
Please visit our web site catalog at
www.schifferbooks.com

This book may be purchased from the publisher.
Include $3.95 for shipping. Please try your bookstore first.
We are always looking for people to write books on new and
related subjects. If you have an idea for a book please contact
us at the above address.
You may write for a free catalog.

In Europe, Schiffer books are distributed by
Bushwood Books
6 Marksbury Avenue
Kew Gardens
Surrey TW9 4JF England
Phone: 44 (0) 20-8392-8585; Fax: 44 (0) 20-8392-9876
E-mail: Bushwd@aol.com
Free postage in the UK. Europe: air mail at cost.

Dedication

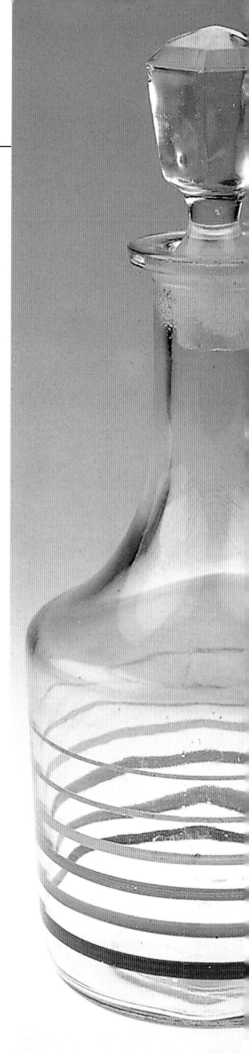

Over the years I have come to appreciate the little things in life. I try to live in the world and not on it. Too often people get so involved in the everyday "survival" that they forget what is really important. When I decided to write books on Anchor Hocking glassware, monetary rewards were not the goal . . . they still aren't! I knew right from the start that authors don't get rich monetarily. They do become rich in what is really important . . . people. My rewards for writing have been the numerous friends I have made over the last four years. One in particular is at the forefront of my mind. Ottis Lee was initially a bidding rival on eBay. We both collected Royal Ruby glassware and it was a fight to the finish to see who would win the prize. I never did keep score, but Ottis said I was the winner on most of the auctions. I finally met Ottis and his wife Mary at the National Depression Glass Show in Little Rock, Arkansas, in July of 1999. Ottis and Mary made the long trip from Fort Worth, Texas, just to meet his eBay adversary. I was there selling my Royal Ruby books and displaying glassware. On the first day of the show, up walks this tall, lanky individual who I would expect to see rocking on the front porch of the local filling station watching the world pass by. That was my first contact with Ottis and it was destined to change my life forever. We spent the next couple of days discussing our glass collections, eBay bidding strategies, and what we figured would be the next "hot" glass pattern to collect. We were collectors with identical missions in life. That was two glorious days spent with a great friend and fellow glass collector.

In March 2000, I was delighted to see Ottis again at the Tulsa Depression Glass Show. Once again we talked about glass, eBay auctions, the progress on the Anchor Hocking Glass Museum I am building and about life in general. The crowning event was the dinner at the Olive Garden restaurant on Saturday night. Approximately fifteen collectors went to dinner and had a great time. I was lucky to have Ottis and Mary sit next to Barb (my fiancé at the time) and me. We sat at one end of the table as if we were in a world of our own. That night was the essence of my personal reward for venturing into the writing world. I had a truly great friend. Most people would question my use of the word "friend" for someone I had just met. Even though our relationship was brief, Ottis was a kind, giving person who was always ready to lend a warm hand. He was funny, polite, easy-going, and what I wanted in a friend!

I was totally devastated to learn that Ottis had left us!!! I know in my heart that he has to be in Heaven at the right hand of God. I feel honored knowing him and I wanted to dedicate this book to his memory. He exemplifies everything I want to be . . a dedicated glass collector, a good Christian, and a truly great friend. Ottis, we will all miss you! Do save a place at the table in Heaven so, when we join you, we can continue to swap stories!

Acknowledgments

I want to thank three very special people in my life. First and foremost is my wife Barbara. She has my "rock" and stood beside me during all the glass buying trips, packing and unpacking glass, photo sessions, and stress of writing several books. Next, I would also like to thank Susan Shaub for helping move glassware for four days during the marathon photo session for the decorated pitcher and glass books. Finally, I want to thank Bruce Waters for all his help in photographing the books, sorting the slides, and designing the book covers. Without these three people to help me, none of the books would have been possible. I thank them for their support and technical expertise.

We shot over 2,100 photographs in three days at my home in Texas. This feat required the transport of over 2,000 pieces of glass and 250-boxed sets from locations in the house to the photographic setup. After the photo session was over, all the glass was intact and nothing was broken! Unfortunately, as we were commending ourselves on this feat, I kicked a glass and it shattered into a million pieces. Still, one broken glass is a small price to pay for three books!

Contents

Foreword

I had a difficult time trying to decide how to organize this book to make it "user friendly." I finally decided to divide the book into three volumes: (1) one volume to cover the earlier years (approximately 1920 through 1950), (2) a second volume to cover the Fire King years (approximately 1950 to 1970) and (3) a final volume to cover everything made until the present day. I also tried to group the pitchers into decoration categories such as pitcher with stripes, juice pitchers, frosted pitchers, etc., since many of the decorations are not listed in catalogs and have no company decoration designation. In the later years, Anchor Hocking used three general styles of pitchers: (1) the 86 oz. upright pitcher, (2) the Finlandia style pitcher, and (3) the Chateau style pitcher. Some of the styles have been used for over 20 years and may still be in use. These three pitcher styles were originally made of colored glass without any decoration. In later years, the company added etching or enameled decorations. Then, the pitcher was given a name indicative of the added decoration and not the basic shape or style of the pitcher.

Introduction

Pricing

The prices in the book are only a guide. They are retail prices for mint condition glassware. Several factors will have an effect on glassware prices: regional availability, depth and consistency in coloring, the presence or absence of Anchor Hocking markings in the glass or as paper labels, and relative rarity of the piece. Certain items will command higher prices if they are sets in the original packaging. I would also consider labeled pieces (paper or marks embedded in the glass) to command a 10 to 20 percent increase in price over unmarked pieces. Prices will drop considerably for glassware that is chipped, scratched, cracked, or deformed. No matter what any reference book states, the bottom line is . . .

Glassware is only worth what someone is willing to pay for it!

Measurements

I have tried to make this reference book as "user friendly" as possible. Too many times I have been in an antique shop and spotted a tumbler I wanted. The reference book I was using said this was a 12 oz. tumbler. Without a container of liquid and measuring cup I would have no way to actually determine if the tumbler held 12 ounces. I would rather know the tumbler is 5 inches high with a top diameter of 3 inches. This I can measure with a ruler. Unless otherwise noted, the measurements listed in the book are the height of the item. Realize, throughout the production of certain glassware items, the mold dimensions did vary. The measurements in the book are the actual measurements made on each piece of glassware pictured.

Resources Available to Collectors

llectors today have a great variety of resources available. With the advent of the "electronic age," collecting capabilities have been greatly expanded. I can honestly state that this book would not have been possible without using the vast resources available, especially on the internet. Below I have listed the resources collectors can use for locating antiques and glassware; however, realize this list is not all-inclusive.

Internet Resources: Without leaving the comfort of your home or office, you can search worldwide for items to add to your collection. Presently, there are both antique dealers and auctions services on the internet.

eBay Auction Service: The eBay Auction Service provides a continually changing source of items. This internet service contains over 3,000,000 items in 371 categories. Internet users can register as both buyers and/or sellers. The majority of the items remain on the "auction block" for seven days. You can search the auction database for specific items. A list of items will be presented following the search. For example, you might want to find a Fire King Jadeite vase made by Anchor Hocking. Because the seller enters the item's description in the database, you often have to anticipate how the item is described. Don't limit the searches. In this case, you might have to search under Jadeite, hocking, fireking (no space), fire king (with the space), or vase to find the item you want.

Internet Antique Malls: There are several internet antique malls I have found to be extremely useful in locating glassware. Each mall contains numerous individual dealers with items for sale. The malls I used are listed below:

1. TIAS Mall – (http://www.tias.com/)
2. Collector Online Mall – (http://www.collectoronline.com)
3. Facets Mall – (http://www.facets.net/facets/shopindx.htm)
4. Depression Era Glass and China Megashow –

(http://www.glassshow.com/)
5. Cyberattic Antiques and Collectibles – (http://cyberattic.com/)

Glass shows, antique shops, and flea markets: All collectors still enjoy searching the deep dark crevices of the local antique shops and flea markets. Many of the best "finds" in my personal collection were located in flea markets and "junk" shops. Most of the dealers in glass shows have a good working knowledge of glassware, so "real finds" are not too plentiful.

Periodicals: Both the *Depression Glass Magazine* and *The Daze, Inc.* are periodicals which will greatly enhance your collecting abilities. Along with the numerous advertisements for glassware, there are informative articles on all facets of collecting glassware.

Word of Mouth: This is one resource so often overlooked. Let others know what you are looking for. Consider expanding you search by including friends, relatives, and other collectors. This book could not have been written without the help of many fellow collectors.

Do not limit you collecting to only one resource. Remember the items you seek are out there . . . somewhere!

Request for Additional Information

I am always seeking information concerning Anchor Hocking's glassware production. Much of the information about the company is not available in a printed format. This book will undoubtedly be updated and it is imperative new information be made available to collectors. If you have any information you would like to share with the "collector world," please contact me at the following address:

Philip L. Hopper
6126 Bear Branch
San Antonio, Texas 78222
E-mail: rrglass@satx.rr.com
Please be patient if you need a response. I am not in the glassware business. I am a military officer first and a collector the rest of the time. I will make every effort to provide prompt feedback on you inquiries. Include a self-addressed, stamped envelope if you desire a written response.

History of Anchor Hocking

Anchor Hocking first came into existence when Isaac J. Collins and six friends raised $8,000 to buy the Lancaster Carbon Company when it went into receivership in 1905. The company's facility was known as the Black Cat from all the carbon dust. Mr. Collins, a native of Salisbury, Maryland, had been working in the decorating department of the Ohio Flint Glass Company when this opportunity arose. Unfortunately, the $8,000 that was raised was not sufficient to purchase and operate the new company, so Mr. Collins enlisted the help of Mr. E. B. Good. With a check for $17,000 provided by Mr. Good, one building, two day-tanks, and 50 employees, Mr. Collins was able to begin operations at the Hocking Glass Company.

The company, named for the Hocking River near which the plant was located, made and sold approximately $20,000 worth of glassware in the first year. Production was expanded with the purchase of another day-tank. This project was funded by selling $5,000 in stock to Thomas Fulton, who was to become the Secretary-Treasurer of Hocking Glass Company.

Just when everything seemed to be going well, tragedy struck the company in 1924 when the Black Cat was reduced to ashes by a tremendous fire. Mr. Collins and his associates were not discouraged. They managed to raise the funding to build what is known as Plant 1 on top of the ashes of the Black Cat. This facility was specifically designed for the production of glassware. Later in that same year, the company also purchased controlling interest in the Lancaster Glass Company (later called Plant 2) and the Standard Glass Manufacturing Company with plants in Bremen and Canal Winchester, Ohio.

The development of a revolutionary machine that pressed glass automatically would save the company when the Great Depression hit. The new machine raised production rates from 1 item per minute to over 30 items per minute. When the 1929 stock market crash hit, the company responded by developing a 15-mold machine that could produce 90 pieces of blown glass per minute. This allowed the company to sell tumblers "two for a nickel" and survive the depression when so many other companies vanished.

Hocking Glass Company entered the glass container business in 1931 with the purchase of 50% of the General Glass Company, which in turn acquired Turner Glass Company of Winchester, Indiana. In 1934, the company developed the first one-way, nonrefundable beer bottle.

Anchor Hocking Glass Corporation came into existence on December 31, 1937 when the Anchor Cap and Closure Corporation and its subsidiaries merged with the Hocking Glass Company. The Anchor Cap and Closure

Corporation had closure plants in Long Island City, New York, and Toronto, Canada, and glass container plants in Salem, New Jersey, and Connellsville, Pennsylvania.

Anchor Hocking Glass Corporation continued to expand into other areas of production such as tableware, closure and sealing machinery, and toiletries and cosmetic containers through the expansion of existing facilities and the purchase of Baltimore, Maryland, based Carr-Lowry Glass Company and the west coast Maywood Glass. In the 1950s, the corporation established the Research and Development Center in Lancaster, purchased the Tropical Glass and Container Company in Jacksonville, Florida, and built a new facility in San Leandro, California, in 1959.

In 1962, the company built a new glass container plant in Houston, Texas, while also adding a second unit to the Research and Development Center, known as the General Development Laboratory. In 1963, Zanesville Mold Company in Ohio became an Anchor Hocking Corporation subsidiary. The company designed and manufactured mold equipment for Anchor Hocking.

The word "Glass" was dropped from the company's name in 1969 because the company had evolved into an international company with an nearly infinite product list. They had entered the plastic market in 1968 with the acquisition of Plastics Incorporated in St. Paul, Minnesota. They continued to expand their presence in the plastic container market with the construction of a plant in Springdale, Ohio. This plant was designed to produce blown mold plastic containers. Anchor Hocking Corporation entered the lighting field in September 1970 with the purchase of Phoenix Glass Company in Monaca, Pennsyl-vania. They also bought the Taylor, Smith & Taylor Company, located in Chester, West Virginia, to make earthenware, fine stoneware, institutional china dinnerware, and commemorative collector plates.

Over the years, several changes occurred in the company. Phoenix Glass Company was destroyed by fire on 15 July 1978; Shenango China (New Castle, Pennsylvania) was purchased in 28 March 1979; Taylor, Smith & Taylor was sold on 30 September 1981; and on 1 April 1983, the company decided to divest its interest in the Glass Container Division to an affiliate of the Wesray Corporation. The Glass Container Division was to be known as the Anchor Glass Container Corporation with seven manufacturing plants and its office in Lancaster, Ohio.

The Newell Corporation acquired the Anchor Hocking Corporation on 2 July 1987. With this renewed influx of capital, several facilities were upgraded and some less profitable facilities were either closed or sold. The Clarksburg, West Virginia, facility was closed in November 1987, Shenango China was sold on 22 January 1988, and Carr-Lowry Glass was sold on 12 October 1989. Today, Anchor Hocking enjoys the financial backing and resources as one of the eighteen decentralized Newell Companies that manufacture and market products in four basic markets: house wares, hardware, home furnishings, and office products. You may recognize such familiar Newell Companies such as Intercraft, Levolor Home Fashions, Anchor Hocking Glass, Goody Products, Anchor Hocking Specialty Glass, Sanford, Stuart Hall, Newell Home Furnishings, Amerock, BerzOmatic, or Lee/Rowan.

Identification Marks

Over the years Anchor Hocking has used several identification marks to mark their glassware. In 1980, the company issued a limited edition 75th anniversary ashtray, pictured below, which portrays the corporate identification marks. During the photographing, the marks on the ashtray were blackened with a magic marker so they would show up when photographed. Originally, when the Hocking Glass Company was established in 1905, the company used the mark seen on the left side of the ashtray. This mark was used from 1905 until 1937, when it was replaced by the more familiar anchor over H mark (center of ashtray) to illustrate the merger of the Hocking Glass Company and the Anchor Cap Company. Finally, in October 1977, the company adopted a new symbol (right side of the ashtray), an anchor with a modern, contemporary appearance to further the new corporate identity.

Catalog Identification

Anchor Hocking used a series of numbers and letters to denote glassware identification in the catalogs. Starting with a basic design number, the company placed a letter (prefix) in front of the number to denote the color and cut or glass type selection. The following is a listing of the letter designations generally used throughout the catalogs:

No prefix - Crystal
E - Forest Green
F - Laser Blue
H - Crystal Fire King
J - Cut Glass
L - Luster Shell
N - Honey Gold
R - Royal Ruby
T - Avocado
Y - Spicy Brown
W - White

For pitchers and glasses, each item of a particular pattern was given its own designation to indicate the capacity. Below are the common capacity designations:

63 - 6 oz. fruit juice
65 - 11 oz. tumbler
69 - 15 oz. iced tea
92 - 19 oz. large iced tea
93 - 22 oz. giant iced tea
3375 - 32 oz. giant sized ice tea
86 - 86 oz. capacity of pitcher

The patterns were also given specific designations. Below is a listing of some common Forest Green pattern designations:

325 - Colonial Lady
351 - Leaf Design
352 - Polka Dots
5612 - Spinning Wheel and Churn
5613 - Wild Geese
5614 - Floral and Diamond
5615 - Gazelle
5705 - Gold and White Vintage
5807 - White Lace

Putting this all together, the #E92/5612 would indicate a Forest Green tumbler (E), 19 oz. large iced tea (92), in the Spinning Wheel and Churn pattern (5612).

What is Glass?

Most people were taught that there are three states of matter in the universe: solids, liquids, and gasses. So, how would you classify glass? People, who have hit a car window during an automobile accident or leaned on a glass counter in a department store would say that glass is a solid. Well, that is not the case. A solid, by definition, is any material that retains its shape without being contained. Glass is constantly flowing and does not retain it shape. Now, the process is extremely slow. Glass is termed a super cooled liquid because it is solid and molecular motion only ceases when glass is at –459.69 degrees Fahrenheit (absolute zero). At this temperature, which has never been achieved, glass would become a solid. If a substance was a solid, it should have a melting point. There are no melting points listed for glass since it is always a liquid except at absolute zero. When companies process glass, they are not melting the glass; they are only making it more fluid. The hotter the glass gets, the more fluid it becomes.

Have you ever noticed that old glass windows tend to rattle as they get older? They also are wavy in appearance. How does this happen and why are the lines in a window always horizontal? First, since glass is a super cooled liquid that is always in motion, it is being constantly pulled downward by gravity. The process is very, very slow. Over a number of years, the glass begins to form irregular wavy lines on the surface. The top of a pane of glass is becoming thinner and the bottom becoming thicker. Eventually, the glass at the top of the windowpane becomes so thin that it is loose in the frame. Any loud noise, gust of wind or strong movement within the building will cause the top of the windowpane to move and rattle.

Now consider what happens when someone hits a baseball through that old window. After the ball has shattered the windowpane, the top pieces fall out easily. But the bottom pieces remain firmly affixed in the window frame. Over the years, as gravity pulled the glass downward, the thickness of the windowpane was increasing at the bottom edge. This wedged the glass between the putty and window frame. Even with the ball rocketing through the window, the lower portion of the window remained firmly in place while the top pieces fell out of the frame. Even in the horror movies you see people injured by the glass falling out of the top of the frame while the bottom pieces remain firmly in place. They are not using old windows, they just happen to be recreating what would really happen when an old window is broken.

Fire King Glass Versus Regular Glass

Confusion exists over the differences between Fire King and regular soda lime glass. Fire King is not a brand name for glass, it is a type of glass. Fire King is borosilicate glass made by melting a combination of sand with sodium borate. This glass melts at a temperature about 200 degrees Fahrenheit higher than regular soda lime glass. Borosilicate glass is noted for its very low expansion coefficient. It can be used in ovens for cooking, but not on the stove. During the making of Fire King glass, the furnace emits boron compounds that are environmentally "unfriendly" and corrosive to the brick lining in the glass furnaces. For these reasons, Fire King glass is reasonable expensive to produce.

What we know as "regular" glass is a melted mixture of sand, soda ash (anhydrous sodium carbonate), and limestone (calcium carbonate). It has an expansion rate three times that of borosilicate glass. When heated unevenly (i.e., on a stove), the heated portions near the hot stove elements will expand at three times the rate of the unheated portions. This will cause internal stress points to form in the glass. If the stress becomes sufficient, cracking will occur.

Anchor Hocking Glass Museum

Since I started collecting Anchor Hocking glass I have always heard and read about the infamous "morgue." The "morgue" is located at Anchor Hocking's Lancaster, Ohio, plant. The "morgue" contains examples of glass production spanning many years. I have toured the area on more than one occasion and found it to be very interesting. Access to the "morgue" is severely limited because the area is located in the middle of the production facility. The majority of the pieces of glass in the "morgue" are later production pieces and generally only cover production at the Lancaster, Ohio, plant. The glass is displayed on large shelves on rollers. The glass is crowded, unlabelled, not well organized, and very difficult to observe because the roller shelves can only be separated by about three to four feet. I did not see examples of Anchor Hocking's bottle production, but there are examples of glass produced in other divisions of the company. Overall, it was an interesting piece of Anchor Hocking history to see and an exciting experience.

I think it is important for everyone to actually see the glass that Anchor Hocking produced, so I am building a facility to display my collection of over 8,000 pieces of Anchor Hocking glass. With a couple of exceptions, all the glass pictured in my books will be on display in the museum. There will also be some unknown pieces of Anchor Hocking glass on display that will be featured in upcoming books. The museum will not have regular hours of operation. The collection can be viewed by calling the museum on a phone number that will be published once the museum is officially open. I designed and built the facility over the last 18 months and included a long porch that will have rocking chairs for visitors to sit in and relax. We are already planning a second facility to display an extensive collection of boxed sets, more glass, and company catalogs. Eventually, we will also add a photo studio to the facility.

This is the catalog page listing the plain Finlandia style pitcher. The catalogs list Finlandia in Laser Blue, Crystal, Honey Gold, Aquamarine, and Avocado Green.

A

B

C

D

E

F

G

H

I

J

K

The same catalog also lists the decorated Finlandia style pitcher with floral decorations as Misty Daisy. The Misty Daisy decoration was applied to all the colors of the plain Finlandia design pitcher.

Common stock certificate for the Anchor Cap Corporation.

Common stock certificate for the Anchor Cap Corporation.

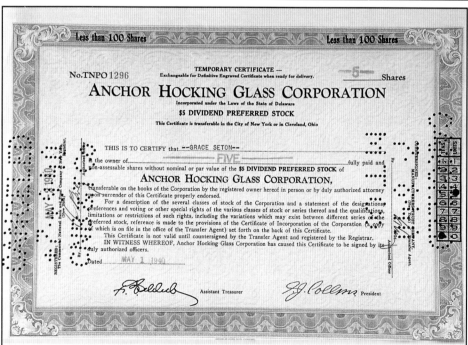

Common stock certificate for the Anchor Hocking Glass Corporation.

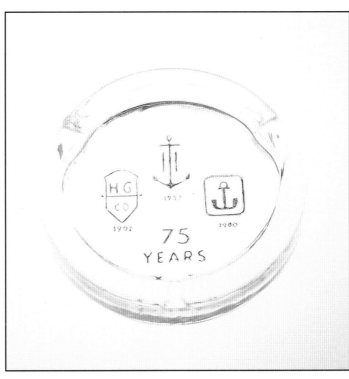

The three identification marks used by the company.

The mark of the Hazel Atlas Glass Company is often confused as being a mark for Anchor Hocking Glass Company. If this were the mark for Anchor Hocking, the letters would be reversed with the capital "A" over the lower case "h".

CHAPTER ONE

Simple Methods to Identify Anchor Hocking Pitchers

There are some very simple ways to distinguish Anchor Hocking pitchers from those of other glass companies. Most of the pitchers in this book were identified from the extensive library of company catalogs that I have. When the particular pitcher cannot be located in the catalogs, I use another method. While the companies did tend to copy decorations applied to the glass, there are some very pronounced differences in the shape or design of the pitcher itself.

Left to right: Bartlett-Collins Satin finish 80 oz. ice lip jug pitcher; Anchor Hocking Finlandia design pitcher. While both of the pitchers are similar in height, there are two distinct differences. First, the Bartlett-Collins pitcher is flat on the bottom while the Anchor Hocking Finlandia design pitcher has a 3/8" pedestal. Second, the Bartlett-Collins pitcher's sides spread out more near the base, while the Anchor Hocking Finlandia pitcher's sides are more vertical.

Left to right: Anchor Hocking 86 oz. upright pitcher; Bartlett-Collins 80 oz. ice lip jug Decoration #103 made in 1955. You will notice that the sides of the Anchor Hocking pitcher are more curved than the Bartlett-Collins pitcher. Also, the shoulder of the Anchor Hocking pitcher has a distinct series of flat spots while the Bartlett-Collins pitcher shoulder is smooth.

Left to right: Bartlett-Collins #100 ball jug Decoration #18 made in 1942; Anchor Hocking tilt ball pitcher; Bartlett-Collins #100 ball jug Decoration #377 made from 1938 to 1940. There are three distinct differences between the pitchers from the two companies. First, the Anchor Hocking tilt ball pitcher has circular rings around the neck. These rings are not found on Bartlett-Collins ball jugs. Second, the handle of an Anchor Hocking pitcher curves farther away from the pitcher. Finally, the neck of the Anchor Hocking pitcher is about 50 percent taller than Bartlett-Collins pitchers.

Left to right: Anchor Hocking 86 oz. upright pitcher; Hazel Atlas 80 oz. jug number 52X-1816 decoration #1033 made from 1938 to 1939. You will notice that the Hazel Atlas pitcher is about ¾" taller than the Anchor Hocking pitcher, it is thinner in diameter, and the shoulder has a totally different shape.

Many collectors confuse Anchor Hocking and Hazel Atlas pitchers, especially these two. The most noticeable difference is the multiple lines that circle around the neck, shoulder area, and base of the Hazel Atlas pitcher. Anchor Hocking pitchers were not made with this multiple line design.

Hazel Atlas beverage sets were even packed in boxes similar to Anchor Hocking's boxes.

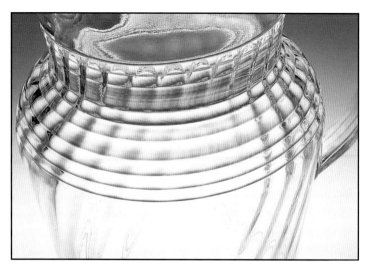

Close-up of the multiple lines that circle the neck and shoulder area of many Hazel Atlas pitchers.

Left to right: Anchor Hocking 86 oz. upright pitcher; Federal #175 85 oz. decoration #8580 South Seas pitcher made in 1953. There are two basic differences to look for here. First, the handle of the Federal pitcher is horizontal at the top, while the Anchor Hocking pitcher's handle is completely curved from top to bottom. Second, the sides of the Federal pitcher are more curved so the base is smaller in diameter than the Anchor Hocking pitcher.

Left to right: Anchor Hocking 86 oz. upright pitcher; Federal #177 85 oz. decoration #7890 Windows pitcher made in 1963. There are four distinct differences to observe. First, the handle of the Federal pitcher is horizontal at the top. Second, there is a distinct line around the shoulder of the Federal pitcher. Third, the base of the Federal pitcher has a ½" pedestal. Finally, the sides of the Federal pitcher are basically straight while the Anchor Hocking pitcher's sides are gently curved.

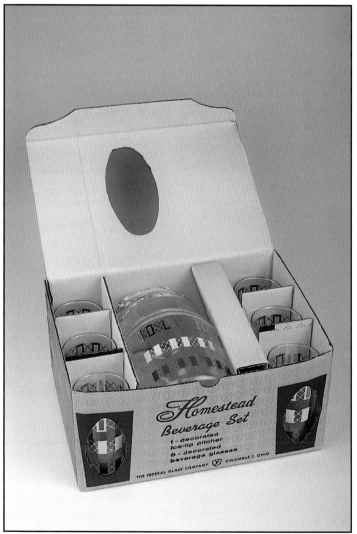

The Federal Windows decoration beverage set in the original box.

Left to right: Federal 32 oz. juice pitcher; Anchor Hocking 36 oz. juice pitcher; Federal 32 oz. juice pitcher. While both the Federal and Anchor Hocking juice pitchers have the same general shape and height, there are two distinct differences. First, the upper portion of the Anchor Hocking pitcher's handle is horizontal while the Federal pitcher's handle is completely curved from top to bottom. Second, the Federal pitcher has a smaller diameter than the Anchor Hocking pitcher.

Since most Anchor Hocking and Libbey pitchers are almost impossible to tell apart, boxed sets become increasingly important in identification. The yellow frosted pitcher looks identical to the Anchor Hocking 86 oz. upright pitcher. Unless you found the frosted pitcher in the original box you might not know who made it. Since Libbey and Anchor Hocking pitchers and glasses are so similar, be sure to look at the glasses for clues. Most Libbey glasses have an upper case cursive "L" in the glass. Most of the Libbey gold designed glasses are marked with this symbol. The same holds true with most Hazel Atlas sets. While the pitchers are not generally marked, the glasses usually have the upper case "H" over the lower case "a" mark.

Left to right: Libbey 32 oz. juice pitcher; Anchor Hocking 36 oz. juice pitcher. Notice that the horizontal area of the handle is on the bottom of the Libbey pitcher but on the top of the Anchor Hocking pitcher. The Libbey pitcher also has a smaller diameter.

Left to right: Anchor Hocking 86 oz. upright pitcher; Libbey 86 oz. upright pitcher. Notice the pitchers are virtually identical with the exception of the applied yellow decoration.

Boxed set of Line Lites. These sets are being sold on the internet as Anchor Hocking products when, in fact, they are not. Anchor Glass Container made these glasses. This is not an Anchor Hocking company. Anchor Glass Container also uses a mark that looks like two "Js" placed back to back. This symbol is mistaken for the Anchor Hocking "anchor over H" symbol used from 1937 to 1977.

Close-up of label on the Line Lites box.

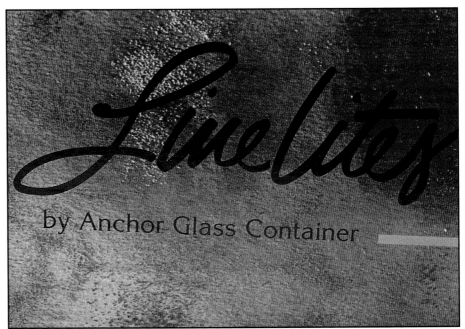

Another set of glasses sold by Anchor Glass Container.

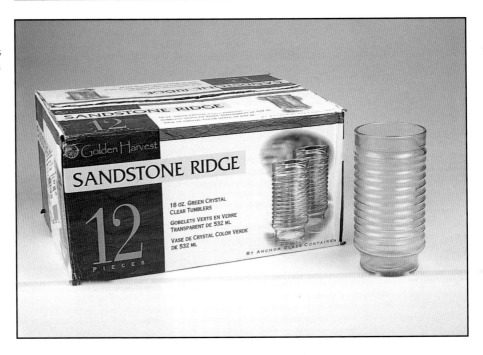

CHAPTER TWO
Mix and Match

Through the years I have been amazed at the combinations of pitchers and glasses that I have discovered. With the advent of companies such as Gay Fad Studio of Lancaster, Ohio, pitchers and glasses from different companies were "married" together to produce some unusual combinations. The Gay Fad Studio hand-painted glassware from several companies and either they, or some other company, sold glass from different companies as sets. Below are some unusual examples.

Macbeth-Evans Corning 80 oz. hand made ice lip chiller with marked 11 oz. 4 ¾" Anchor Hocking straight shell glasses, $75-85 for the entire set.

Marked Anchor Hocking 40 oz. chiller with marked Federal Glass Company 3 ½" glasses, $40-50 for the entire set.

Bartlett-Collins yellow frosted 80 oz. ice lip jug with Anchor Hocking 9 oz. 4 7/8" coupette glasses, $30-40 for the entire set.

Two very similar designs for the 9 oz. coupette glasses. Left to right: Anchor Hocking coupette, $2-5; Bartlett-Collins coupette, $2-5.

Notice the small "wafer" of glass just under the bowl of the coupette on the left. This is common on Anchor Hocking stemmed glasses. The Bartlett-Collins coupette on the right does not have the wafer.

Mountaineer Glass etched pitcher with Anchor Hocking 5 oz. 3 3/8" Roly Poly juice glasses, $40-50 for the entire set.

Bartlett-Collins ice lip pitcher with marked Anchor Hocking 5 oz. 3 3/8" Roly Poly juice glasses, $50-60 for the entire set. The glasses are marked with the "anchor over H" emblem.

Marked Federal 6 ½" (to the top of the spout) cocktail shaker with Anchor Hocking 3 ½ oz. 3" cocktail glasses.

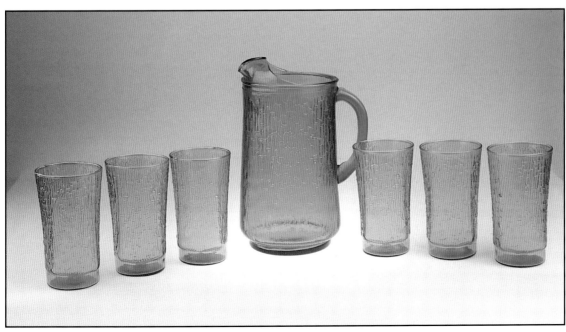

This was not the only "mix and match" process going on during these years. Even Anchor Hocking mixed patterns to produce some unusual sets. Above is a Finlandia style pitcher that is covered with the Pagoda design surface. The set was not sold with Finlandia style glasses, but sold with Pagoda water glasses.

CHAPTER THREE
Not All Hand-Painted
Glass Was Made by the Gay Fad Studio

This photo was supposed to have been taken in the Gay Fad Studio. Notice all the different decorations and types of glass sold by the studio.

Over the years collectors have come to treasure hand-painted glassware. Probably the most notable company to hand-paint glass was the Gay Fad Studio of Lancaster, Ohio. When most collectors see hand-painted items, they naturally conclude the glass was painted at the Gay Fad Studio. Unfortunately, this is not always true. There were many art studios besides the Gay Fad Studio that hand-painted glassware. I have found pieces of glass with labels from Hansetta-Artware Company of New York, New York, Washington Company of Washington, Pennsylvania, United Glass Industries (location unknown), and Imperial (location unknown). Information about these art studios and companies is very limited due to their small size, brief history, and limited production. Undoubtedly, there are others that will surface in time.

While most people associate the Gay Fad Studio with hand-painted glassware, the studio was also responsible for producing many machine-decorated items. Many of the decorations are so intricate that they could only have been done by machine.

Hansetta-Artware Company hand-painted pitcher and glasses. The set consisted of a Federal 85 oz. pitcher and six Anchor Hocking 3 ½ oz. 3" cocktail glasses, $75-100 for the set with label.

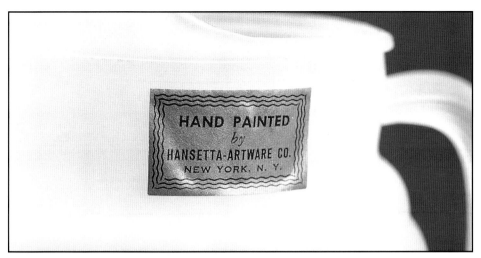

Close-up of the Hansetta-Artware Company label.

Hansetta-Artware Company hand-painted pitcher and glasses. The set consisted of an Anchor Hocking 40 oz. juice pitcher and six Baltic 5 oz. 3 ¾" juice glasses, $75-100 for the set with the label.

Hansetta-Artware Company hand-painted pitcher and glasses. The set consisted of a Federal 85 oz. ice lip pitcher with six Anchor Hocking 11 oz. 4 ¼" straight shell glasses, $75-100 for the set with the label.

Photo of Gay Fad Studio machine decorated pitcher and glasses. The set consisted of an Anchor Hocking 86 oz. upright pitcher with the 15 oz. 5 ¼" straight shell glasses, $75-85 for the set with the Gay Fad marking.

Close-up of the Gay Fad signature on the pitcher.

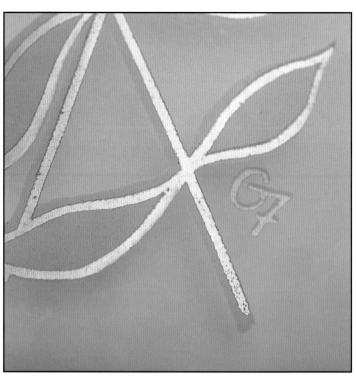

The Gay Fad marking on the juice pitcher was only the "GF" initials.

Photo of 40 oz. juice pitcher with the same design as the 86 oz. upright pitcher, $25-35 for the pitcher alone.

Box containing a Gay Fad 7-Piece Juice Set, $80-100 for the complete set, $25-30 for the box only.

The 7-Piece Juice Set removed from the box. The set consisted of a Federal 36 oz. juice jug #2604 with six 3" glasses with machine applied designs, $60-70 for the set without the box.

Center right: Another 7-Piece Beverage Set sold by Gay Fad Studio, $100-125 for the complete set, $25-30 for the box only.

Center left: Photo of a Christmas glass from Gay Fad Studio. The design was applied by machine to a Hazel Atlas 3" glass, $5-7.

The 7-Piece Beverage Set was hand-painted by United Glass Industries, yet it was sold in a box marked with Gay Fad Studio. The set consisted of one 86 oz. pitcher and six 10 oz. 5" tapered glasses, $80-100 for the set without the box.

Left: Close-up of the United Glass Industries label. I have been unable to find out where the company was located or how long it was in business. If you have any information about the company, its history, or products, please let me know.

Right: Close-up of the United Glass Industries label.

Photo of United Glass Industries hand-painted pitcher and glasses. The set consisted of the Anchor Hocking 36 oz. juice pitcher with six Anchor Hocking 5 oz. 3 3/8" Roly Poly fruit juice glasses, $80-100 for the set with the label.

Photo of United Glass Industries hand-painted pitcher and glasses with the butterfly design. The set consisted of an Anchor Hocking 36 oz. juice pitcher with six Anchor Hocking 6 oz. 3 ¾" juice glasses, $80-100 for the set with the label.

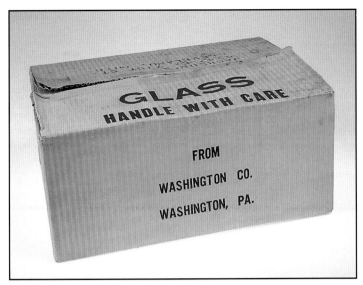

Boxed Beverage Set made by Washington Company of Washington, Pennsylvania, $100-125 for the complete set with the box, $30-35 for the box only. The Washington Company did hand-paint and color treat glassware from many different companies, but mainly Hazel Atlas. Some of the more common pieces were pitcher sets, salad sets, and serving pieces. The company employed about a dozen women as artists. Like the Gay Fad Studio, they did not produce any glassware. The company was located near the Hazel Atlas plant number 1. The Washington Company was in business from the late 1940s until the late 1960s and they may have been a subsidiary of Hazel Atlas, although as of this writing that association remains unclear.

The 7-Piece Beverage Set consisted of one Anchor Hocking 86 oz. upright pitcher and six 10 oz. 5" tapered glasses, $80-100 for the set with the label.

Left: Close-up of the Washington Company label.

Right: This hand-painted Royal Ruby ivy ball brings up an interesting point. There may be yet another company that hand-painted pitchers and glasses, as well as Royal Ruby items. This is the only piece of glass I have found with this label. If you have any information about the company, please contact me.

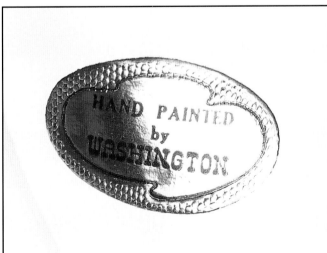

CHAPTER FOUR
Cracking in Anchor Hocking Pitchers

You may have noticed that Anchor Hocking pitchers, especially the pitchers made prior to 1970, may have cracks at the base of the handles. When glass cools in an open environment (not in a controlled furnace or lehr), it has a tendency to cool unevenly. The thicker portions of the pitcher (i.e., the handle) retain the heat longer. This uneven cooling may cause stress points to form in the glass. The stress can only be relieved in two ways. You can reheat the pitcher and control and extend the cooling process to eliminate the stress points. If that was not done, glass will inherently relieve the stress points through the second method of stress relief . . . cracking. Most of the pitchers produced by Anchor Hocking were allowed to air cool, thereby promoting uneven cooling and some handle cracking. Since many of the cracks are very difficult to see unless viewed under strong illumination, cracked pitchers may have been sold to the public by mistake. The cracks did not affect the use of the pitcher since many of the pitchers were used for over 50 years without the handle falling off or the pitcher leaking.

Cracked handle on Tree of Life design pitcher produced in 1933.

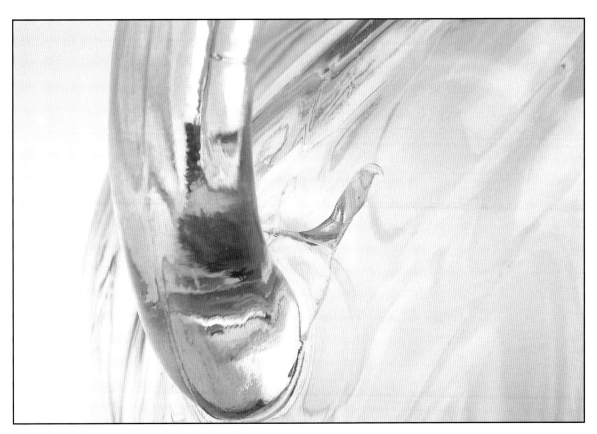

Cracked handle on Swirl design tilt ball pitcher produced in the 1950s.

Cracked handle on a Lido (Milano) design Laser Blue pitcher produced in the 1970s. With the darker colored pitchers, the cracks may be very difficult to see.

CHAPTER FIVE

Miscellaneous Pitchers

Anchor Hocking made a myriad of pitcher designs over the years; however, many of the designs were never listed in catalogs or sales brochures. I have observed most of the designs listed in this chapter when I visited the "morgue" at the Lancaster, Ohio, plant. Hopefully, in the future I will be able to find some definitive documentation to name the patterns.

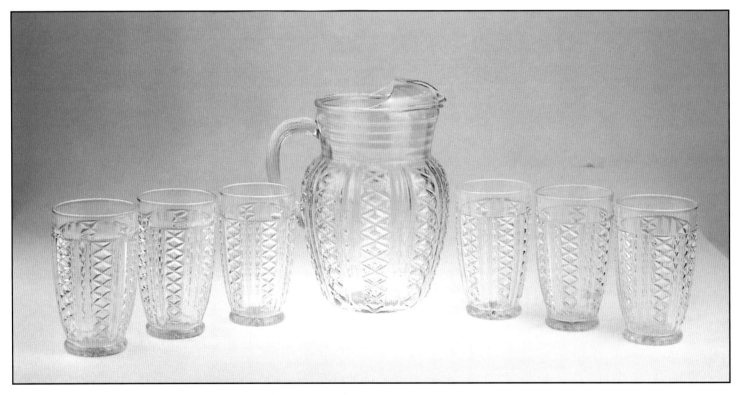

Diamond Line 80 oz. pitcher and six 14 oz. 5 ¼" glasses, $50-75 for the pitcher, $15-20 for each glass.

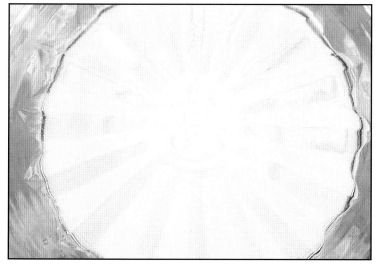

Top: Diamond Line 60 oz. juice pitcher and six 6 oz. 4" juice glasses, $50-65 for the pitcher, $10-12 for each glass.

Center: The Crystal Diamond Line glasses come in three sizes. Left to right: 14 oz. glass, 5 ¼", $15-20; 9 oz. glass, 4", $12-15; 6 oz. glass, 4", $10-12.

Some of the Diamond Line glasses are marked with the familiar "anchor over H" emblem on the bottom. These glasses would command a 50% increase in price over the unmarked glasses.

Pink Diamond Line 60 oz. juice pitcher and four 6 oz. 4" juice glasses, $75-80 for the pitcher, $12-15 for each glass. There is also a pink 80 oz. pitcher (not shown), $80-100.

The pink Diamond Line glasses come in three sizes. Left to right: 14 oz. glass, 5 ¼", $20-25; 9 oz. glass, 4", $15-20; 6 oz. glass, 4", $12-15.

Rare tilt ball pitcher with the High Point pattern, $150-200, with four 5 oz. 3" juice glasses, $10-12 for each glass.

Rare square pitcher with the High Point pattern, $125-150, with six 9 oz. 4" glasses, $15-20 for each glass, and two 5 oz. 3 7/8" glasses, $12-15 for each glass.

High Point pattern applied to an 80 oz. pitcher made from 1927 to 1933, $125-150, with four 10 oz. 4" glasses, $12-15 for each glass, and one 4" bowl, $2-5. I recently found a large 10" crystal bowl with the High Point pattern. Arcoroc of France made the bowl in recent years. The bowl was marked with the company name around the edge of the base of the bowl.

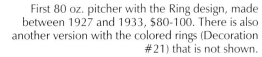

First 80 oz. pitcher with the Ring design, made between 1927 and 1933, $80-100. There is also another version with the colored rings (Decoration #21) that is not shown.

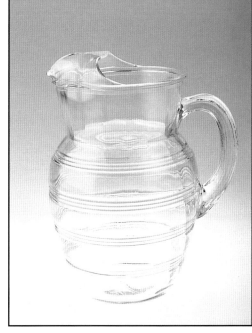

Gold rimmed Ring 80 oz. jug #1380, $50-60, with four 13 oz. 5" glasses, $8-10 for each glass.

Front cover of the Butler Brothers catalog listing Anchor Hocking and Standard Glass items.

The gold-rimmed Ring pitcher was listed in the Butler Brothers catalog, but it was called "Ringed-Optic".

Left to right: crystal Ring 80 oz. jug #1380, $35-50; green Ring 80 oz. jug, $40-50.

Two different sizes, decorations and handle designs on Ring pitchers. Left to right: 80 oz. jug #1380 Decoration #21, $40-50; 56 oz. jug #1354 Decoration #422, $35-50. Notice that the handles have different designs. The Decoration #21 has the colored lines as red, yellow, blue, yellow, and red in that order. The Decoration #422 has the colored lines as black, yellow, red, orange, and black in that order.

The #700/47 7-Piece Arctic Beverage Set made in 1933. The set consists of one 80 oz. pitcher #780 Decoration #165, $50-60, and six #3515 12 oz. 5" ice tea glasses Decoration #165, $10-15 for each glass.

Close-up of the handle. This handle design is indicative of Anchor Hocking pitchers.

The #700/55 7-Piece Polar Bear Beverage Set made in 1933. The set consists of one 80 oz. pitcher #780 Decoration #195, $50-60, and six #3515 12 oz. 5" ice tea glasses (only 4 shown) Decoration #195, $10-15 for each glass.

Another version of the 80 oz. pitcher, $50-60, with one 12 oz. 5" ice tea glass, $10-15.

Another version of the 80 oz. pitcher with enameled flower decorations, $60-80.

Another version of the 80 oz. pitcher with seven etched lines near the top of the body of the pitcher and etched dots at the bottom of the body of the pitcher, $60-80.

This pattern was listed in the Butler Brothers catalog as the Crystal Band and Balloon pattern (Cut #3001). You will notice a myriad of pieces were available in this cut pattern.

The 80 oz. pitcher was modified at the base, while the top and handle remained unchanged. The pink pitcher and glasses are etched with grapes and leaves, $60-75 for the pitcher, $12-15 for each 10 oz. 5" glass.

Another plain pink version of the 80 oz. pitcher, $45-50.

The green pitcher and glasses are etched with grapes and leaves, $60-75 for the pitcher, $12-15 for each 9 oz. 4 ¾" glass.

Relatively rare citrine yellow version of the 80 oz. pitcher, $75-80.

Relatively common green version of the 80 oz. pitcher, $35-50.

The crystal pitcher and glasses with the Gold Band and Hairline decoration, $50-60 for the pitcher, $10-12 for each 11 ½ oz. 5" glass.

Three colors of Pillar Optic pitchers, $40-50 for each color.

Pillar Optic pitcher and six tumblers, $40-50 for the pitcher, $10-12 for each 8 oz. 4" glass.

Top left: Green Pinch Line 80 oz. jug #180 made in 1933, $40-50.

Top right: Tree of life design 80 oz. pitcher made in the early 1930s, $80-100.

Old English decoration 80 oz. pitcher made in the early 1930s,
$60-75, with four 10 oz. 4 ¾" glasses, $10-12 for each glass.

Oriential decoration 80 oz. pitcher made in the early 1930s,
$60-75, with six 10 oz. 4 ¾" glasses, $10-12 for each glass.

Unique 80 oz. pitcher with the Windsor design on the base and etched flowers, $60-75, with six 10 oz. 4" glasses, $10-12 for each glass.

Unique plain 80 oz. pitcher with the Windsor design on the base, $50-60, with four 10 oz. 4" glasses, $10-12 for each glass.

Unique green 80 oz. pitcher with the Windsor design on the base, $70-80, with six 10 oz. 4" glasses, $12-15 for each glass.

Two sizes of Windsor design glasses were available to go with the green pitchers. Left to right: 11 ½ oz. glass, 4 ¾", $20-25; 10 oz. glass, 4", $15-20.

Another unique combination in Anchor Hocking pitchers. This pitcher has the Windsor base design with the Georgian top design, $125-150 for the entire set, $60-75 for the pitcher, $12-15 for each 10 oz. 4" glass.

Another version of the Windsor/Georgian design pitcher with etched flowers, $60-75.

Here is yet another Anchor Hocking oddity. This is the Morocco design pitcher produced in the late 1940s. It is interesting to note that the pitcher was produced without any glasses. The glasses were produced later in the 1980s and in different colors, $60-75 for either color of pitcher.

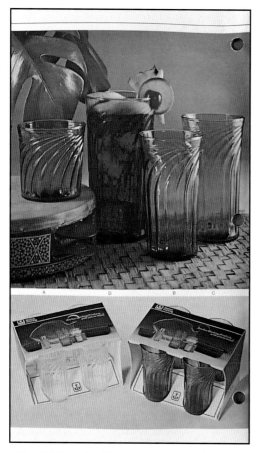

The 1982 catalog listed the Morocco design glasses in Slate.

The 1982 catalog also listed the Morocco design glasses in Crystal and Honey Gold.

Here are some of the Morocco glasses produced in the 1980s. There are actually four sizes of glasses produced in three colors: Slate, Honey Gold, and Crystal.

Anchor Hocking pitcher, design unknown, $75-80, with six 15 oz. 6" footed ice tea glasses, $20-25 for each glass.

Anchor Hocking pitcher, design unknown, made in crystal, $60-75.

The #687 80 oz. pitcher came in three colors, $40-50 for each color. This is not the Old Café pattern, although many people call it Old Café. The bands on Old Café are not all the same width as the bands are on this pitcher design. This pattern was not given a specific name when listed in the catalogs.

One half dozen #687 crystal pitchers in the original box, $250-300. Each pitcher was individually boxed inside the box shown here, $20-25 for the box only.

Unusual pitcher probably made by Anchor Hocking in the 1930s, $40-50. This may have been a transitional or experimental pitcher design.

This style of pitcher was used by Anchor Hocking for many years. Besides the plain pitcher, designs were added to produce such well-known patterns as Cameo. Left to right: plain green pitcher, $25-30; green pitcher with etched grapes, $35-50.

THE STANDARD GLASS MFG. CO., LANCASTER, OHIO

TOPAZ-CUT 6

T-303 - 5 OZ. FRUIT JUICE

T-306 - 10 OZ. TUMBLER

T-308 - 12 OZ. ICE TEA

T-181 - 10 OZ. FOOTED TUMBLER

T-53 SUGAR

T-53 CREAMER

T-112 - 9 OZ. BARREL TUMBLER

T-134 HIGH SHERBET
T-729 - 6" PLATE

T-54 - 57 OZ. JUG

T-179 - CUP
T-729 - SAUCER

T-729 - 6" PLATE

T-23 SHAKERS CHROME N.T.

T-740 - 8" PLATE

Sales brochure from the Standard Glass Manufacturing Company listing the etched grape decoration glassware. Notice that the Standard Glass Manufacturing Company pitcher had a plain, not roped, top edge. The roping was indicative of Anchor Hocking pitchers of the era.

The same design in citrine yellow. Left to right: citrine yellow pitcher
with etched grapes, $45-50; plain citrine yellow pitcher, $35-45.

Three different crystal versions. Left to right: plain crystal pitcher, $20-25; crystal pitcher
with etched grapes, $30-35; crystal pitcher with swirled lines on the inside surface, $35-40.

Frosted version of the pitcher, $40-50. This pitcher has a dog on one side.

The frosted pitcher has the letter "R" etched on the side opposite the dog.

The same pitcher blank was used to make the Crisscross and Cameo pitcher. Left to right: Crisscross design pitcher, $25-30; Cameo pitcher with label, $60-75. The Crisscross design pitcher is also available in crystal (not shown).

Close-up of the Cameo label.

These versions of the pitcher have different top edges. Note the roping around the mouth of the pitcher. Left to right: plain pink pitcher with roped edge, $45-50; pink pitcher with roped edge and etched grapes, $50-60.

Unusual citrine yellow pitcher with the roped edge, $60-75.

Anchor Hocking used other pitcher blanks to produce a variety of different pitcher designs. The Spiral (1928-1930) design pitcher used one of these blanks. Left to right: green Spiral pitcher with narrow roping at the top, $25-35; crystal Spiral pitcher with narrow roping at the top, $25-30; green Spiral pitcher with wide roping at the top, $35-50.

Comparison of the narrow and wide roping found at the top of the Spiral pitchers.

Fan and Flower design pitchers were also made from the same blank as the Spiral pitchers. Left to right: green Fan and Flower pitcher, $30-40; crystal Fan and Flower pitcher, $25-35.

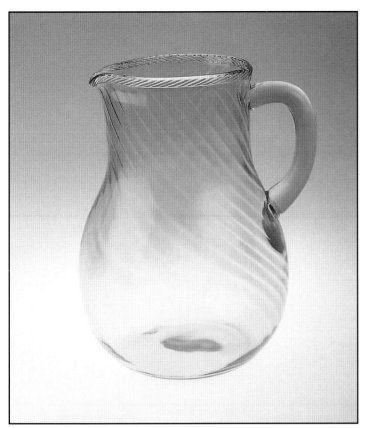

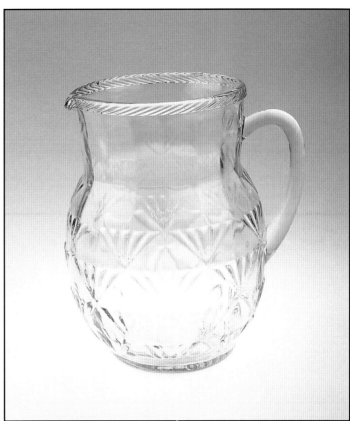

Another common shape for Anchor Hocking pitchers is shown here. As with the previous pitcher shape, this shape was used to make more than one pitcher design. Here is the green Spiral pitcher, $30-40.

This was another design applied to the same pitcher style, $40-50. I have seen this pattern also called Fan and Flower; however, I have not been able to confirm the pattern name in any Anchor Hocking documentation.

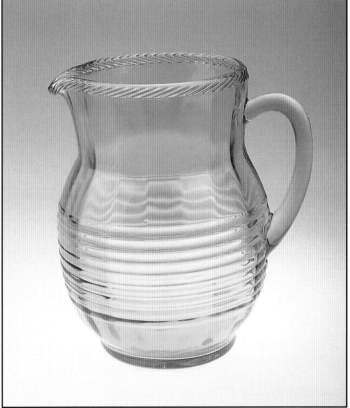

Tree of Life design applied to the same style of pitcher, $50-60.

The Circle pattern (1930) also used the same pitcher design, $40-50.

This pitcher and glass set may have been made by Anchor Hocking. While the pattern of the pieces and the glasses are Anchor Hocking, I am not sure of the pitcher itself. Unlike the previous pitchers, there is a base to the pitcher and the handle is applied and not molded with the body of the pitcher.

Three styles of pitchers made from the same pitcher design blank. Anchor Hocking made the pitchers with the star on the bottom and the roping at the top of the pitcher. Federal Glass probably made those pitchers without the star in the bottom and roping on the top edge since there was a similar pitcher design listed in the Federal Glass catalogs from 1928 to 1930. The Federal pitcher was listed with 6 glasses and called the Optic Iced Tea Set. Left to right: Tree of Life design pitcher, $60-75; plain pitcher, $30-40; pitcher with etched grapes, $50-60. There is also another version of this design with swirls on the inside of the pitcher (not shown).

The Tree of Life design pitcher came with three sizes of glasses. Left to right: pitcher, $50-75; 12 oz. glass, 5 ¼"; $10-12; 8 oz. glass, 4 ½", $10-12; 4 oz. glass, 3 5/8", $8-10.

The Tree of Life pitcher and glasses were originally sold as the 19-Piece Lady Richie British Castle Beverage Ensemble. The set included one pitcher, 12 glasses, and six glass straws, $100-125 for the complete set, $20-25 for the box only.

CHAPTER SIX

Floral Pitchers

Most of the pitchers in this chapter have not been identified in any Anchor Hocking company literature. The pitchers were produced in the 1930s and 1940s when few catalogs or brochures were printed and distributed. The style and shape of the pitchers were Anchor Hocking only. Sets with a pitcher and six glasses will command a premium because they are hard to find. Many of the glasses were broken over years of use and finding the glasses is often very difficult!

Clematis decoration pitcher and glasses, $40-50 for the pitcher, $10-12 for each 11 oz. 4 ¾" glass. There may be two different color combinations for this decoration. The pitcher and glasses were not sold together, they were photographed together to show the two color variations that exist.

Opposite page, bottom: Wildflower decoration pitcher, $35-45, with six 4 ¾" tapered glasses, $10-12 for each glass. This decoration was also applied to a juice pitcher produced in the late 1950s

Left to right: Dogwood decoration 80 oz. ice lip pitcher, $35-45; 11 oz. glass, 4 ¾", $10-12.

This floral decoration pitcher was produced in four distinct versions. Both colored flowers were produced in a clear and frosted version. The clear versions of the pitchers were sold with 4 5/8" glasses and the frosted versions sold with 5 ½" glasses. The clear versions tend to be harder to find and therefore the pitchers would be $40-50 and the glasses $12-15 each.

Frosted floral decoration pitcher $35-45, with six 15 oz. 5 ½" glasses, $10-12 for each glass.

Rose decoration pitcher, $35-45, with four 11 oz. 4 ¾" glasses, $10-12 for each glass.
Notice the green foliage under the flower. There are two foliage versions of this pitcher.

Frosted floral decoration pitcher $35-45, with four 15 oz. 5 ½" glasses, $10-12 for each glass.

Rose decoration pitcher, $35-45, with six 11 oz. 4 ¾" glasses, $10-12 for each glass. Notice the green foliage under the flower. This version is different from the previous pitcher shown.

The Rose decoration pitcher was available with at least two sizes of glasses. Left to right: 15 oz. glass, 5 ½", $12-15; 11 oz. glass, 4 ¾", $10-12.

Orchid decoration pitcher, $35-45, with six 11 oz. 4 ¾" glasses, $10-12 for each glass.

The Orchid decoration pitcher was available with at least two sizes of glasses. Left to right: 15 oz. glass, 5 ½", $12-15; 11 oz. glass, 4 ¾", $10-12.

Petunia decoration pitcher, $35-45, with four 11 oz. 4 ¾" glasses, $10-12 for each glass.

Daffodil decoration pitcher, $35-45, with six 11 oz. 4 ¾" glasses, $10-12 for each glass.

Dogwood decoration pitcher, $35-45, with six 11 oz. 4 ¾" glasses, $10-12 for each glass. There are different colored versions of the flowers on the pitcher.

Another version of the Dogwood design pitcher and glasses, $80-100 for the entire set, $35-45 for the pitcher, $10-12 for each 4 ¾" glass.

These are the "Color Blend" decorated glasses sold to compliment the #790/140 80 oz. pitcher, $10-12 for each glass.

The #790/140 80 oz. water pitcher with petunias, daisies, narcissus, strawberries and currant decorations, $40-50 for the pitcher. The pitcher was made in 1938.

Another pitcher with two color versions and multiple fruits and flowers, $40-50 for each color version.

Three different floral pitchers produced in the late 1930s, $40-50 for each version.

The #790/155 Blossom decoration 80 oz. pitcher produced from 1938 until 1942. The pitcher was sold with the #3519/E 9 ½ oz. 4 ¾" tall tumbler with either red, yellow, orchid, or blue blossoms, $40-50 for the pitcher, $10-12 for each glass.

The #790/136 Red Poppy decoration 80 oz. pitcher produced from 1938 until 1942. The pitcher was sold with either the #3519/136 9 ½ oz. tall tumbler or the #3505/136 12 oz. iced tea, $40-50 for the pitcher, $10-12 for each glass.

Left to right: #700/634 Strawberry decoration 80 oz. pitcher produced in 1948, $40-50; #790/225 Primrose decoration 80 oz. pitcher produced in 1948, $40-50; #66/225 turquoise 11 oz. 4 ¾" tumbler, $10-12. The glasses were available in red, yellow, and turquoise colored flowers.

The #790/229 Dogwood decoration 80 oz. pitcher produced in 1948. The 7-piece set (#700/635) consisted of one pitcher and six #66/229 11 oz. 4 ¾" tumblers (only four pictured), $80-100 for the entire set, $40-50 for the pitcher, $10-12 for each glass.

Three different tulip design pitchers, $40-50 for each design.

Another interesting floral decoration, $80-100 for the entire set, $40-50 for the pitcher, $10-12 for each 11 oz. 4 ¾" glass.

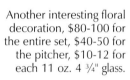

Daisy decoration pitcher, $40-50, with four 11 oz. 4 ¾" glasses, $10-12 for each glass.

Three different floral decoration pitchers, $40-50 for each design.

Yellow Dogwood decoration pitcher, $40-50, with six 11 oz. 4 ¾" glasses, $10-12 for each glass.

Blue Dogwood decoration pitcher, $40-50, with six 11 oz. 4 ¾" glasses, $10-12 for each glass.

71

Red Dogwood decoration pitcher, $40-50, with two 11 oz. 4 ¼" glasses, $10-12 for each glass.

Three more pitchers produced in the 1930s and 1940s, $40-50 for each pitcher.

Three more pitchers produced in the 1930s and 1940s, $40-50 for each pitcher.

Three more pitchers produced in the 1930s and 1940s, $40-50 for each pitcher.

There seems to be an intermediate design pitcher that may have been made by Anchor Hocking. This design looks like a modification of the previous pitchers listed in this chapter. The only difference is the addition of another ridge on the shoulder. The pitcher's handle, ice lip, neck, and base are the same. Unfortunately, I have found some of this style of pitcher with Libbey marked glasses. It was not uncommon for glass companies to mix and match glass, but I am not sure if Anchor Hocking did that for this pattern. More than likely, this style of pitcher was a short-lived version (not often found) until the company produced the 86 oz. plain upright pitcher that it is still producing today, $50-60 for each design.

Anchor Hocking decoration pitchers (?), $50-60, with six 11 oz. 4 ¾" glasses marked with the Libbey capital cursive "L" on the bottom of each glass.

73

Anchor Hocking decoration pitchers (?), $50-60 for each design.

Anchor Hocking decoration pitchers (?). Because the pitcher on the left has Snow White and the Seven Dwarfs, it would command a higher price, $75-100.

CHAPTER SEVEN

Miscellaneous Design Pitchers

Most of the pitchers in this chapter have not been identified in any Anchor Hocking company literature. The pitchers were produced in the 1930s and 1940s when few catalogs or brochures were printed and distributed. The style and shape of the pitchers were Anchor Hocking only. Sets with a pitcher and six glasses will command a premium because they are hard to find. Many of the glasses were broken over years of use and finding the glasses is often very difficult!

The #790/4299 Mexican Pottery decoration 80 oz. pitcher produced from 1933 until 1938. The pitcher was sold with four sizes of tumblers with three different color schemes, $80-100 for the entire set (with six glasses), $40-50 for the pitcher, $10-12 for each glass in any size or color.

Left to right: the 80 oz. #790 pitcher with pictures of cows, $60-80; the 80 oz. #790 pitcher with pictures of Scotty dogs, $80-100.

Maple Leaf decoration 80 oz. pitcher, $40-50, with six 11 oz. 4 ¾" glasses, $10-12 for each glass.

Chinese Ring decoration 80 oz. pitcher, $40-50 for the pitcher in
either color, $10-12 for each 11 oz. 4 ¾" glass.

Left to right: yellow #66/233 11 oz. tumbler, 4 ¾", $10-12; turquoise #66/234 11 oz. tumbler, 4 ¾", $10-12; another
variation of the Chinese Ring decoration 11 oz. tumbler, 4 ¾", $10-12.

Polka Dot decoration 80 oz. pitcher, $40-50.

Candy Stripe decoration 80 oz. pitcher, $40-50, with four 11 oz. 4 ¾" glasses, $10-12 for each glass.

Cherry decoration 80 oz. pitcher, $40-50, with six 11 oz. 4 ¾" glasses, $10-12 for each glass.

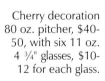

Gazelle decoration 80 oz. pitcher, $200-250 for the entire set (with 12 glasses), $75-100 for the pitcher, $12-15 for each glass. There are three sizes of glasses and four different colored lined versions (red, yellow, blue, and green) for each size. This particular pitcher has the red lines, but there may be other colored lined versions.

Dove decoration 80 oz. pitcher, $60-80, with two 11 oz. 4 ¾" glasses, $10-12 for each glass.

Another Dove decoration 80 oz. pitcher, $60-80, with two 11 oz. 4 ¾" glasses, $10-12 for each glass.

Hand-painted frosted 80 oz. pitcher, $150-200 for the entire set (with 12 glasses), $80-100 for the pitcher, $12-15 for each glass. There are three sizes of glasses and four different fruits for each size. I have not been able to determine which company applied the hand-painted designs. I have seen other pitchers and glasses with the same designs.

Rare 80 oz. pitcher with etched ovals and 22 kt. gold lines, $80-100, with six 11 oz. 4 ¾" glasses, $12-15 for each glass.

Rare 80 oz. pitcher with diamond etched designs, $60-75, with six 9 oz. 4" table tumblers #3361, $12-15 for each glass.

Old English decoration 80 oz. pitcher produced in 1933, $60-75, with four 11 oz. 4 ¼" glasses, $12-15 for each glass. This decoration was first produced in 1933 on a different style of pitcher (shown earlier in this book).

Backside view of the Old English decoration pitcher.

Front side view of the Old English decoration pitcher.

Ship decoration 80 oz. pitcher, $60-75, with six 11 oz. 4 ¾" glasses, $12-15 for each glass.

The red version of the Ship decoration 80 oz. pitcher, $60-75, with two 11 oz. 4 ¾" glasses, $12-15 for each glass.

Another popular Ship decoration 80 oz. pitcher, $60-75, with four 11 oz. 4 ¾" glasses, $12-15 for each glass.

Another popular Ship decoration 80 oz. pitcher, $60-75, with two 11 oz. 4 ¾" glasses, $12-15 for each glass.

Another popular Ship decoration 80 oz. pitcher, $60-75, with four 11 oz. 4 ¾" glasses, $12-15 for each glass. This decoration was used on the 36 oz. and 80 oz. juice pitchers produced in the 1950s and the 86 oz. upright pitcher produced from the early 1950s. Anchor Hocking did modify the waves and leaned the sailboats different directions to create several versions of this popular decoration.

Three more popular Ship decoration 80 oz. pitchers, $60-75 for each design.

CHAPTER EIGHT

Striped Pitchers

Orange striped pitcher produced from 1932 to 1933, $75-100 for
the pitcher, $15-20 for each 4" glass, $10-12 for each glass straw.

This pitcher, the 80 oz. jug Decoration #51, was initially produced by The Lancaster Glass Company from 1932 to 1933. It was sold in a 9-piece set, $75-100 for the pitcher, $25-30 for each 10 oz. 5 ½" footed tumbler.

Close-up of the handle to show that it has a different design than pitcher handles seen on later pieces of glass. This handle was applied after the body of the pitcher was molded. Many of the earlier pitchers were made with these handles.

In 1933, Anchor Hocking introduced this striped pattern called Decoration #97. There is an 80 oz. pitcher to match the pieces shown. Overall, there are 22 different pieces of glass produced in this pattern. They include straight shells, stemmed glasses, footed tumblers, cocktail shaker, ice bucket, plates, sherbets, cups and saucers.

Rare striped version of the 80 oz. pitcher produced in the early 1930s, $60-75. I have located at least two other different striped versions of this pitcher (not shown).

The #780 80 oz. jug produced in 1933. This set consists of one pitcher and six #181 10 oz. 5 ¼" tumblers, $125-150 for the entire set, $50-60 for the pitcher, $15-20 for each glass. There are 30 different pieces of glass in this pattern listed in the catalogs.

The #181 10 oz. 5 ¼" tumbler was also "married" to another pitcher with the same colored lines, but with a slightly different pitcher body design, $150-175 for the entire set, $60-75 for the pitcher, $15-20 for each glass.

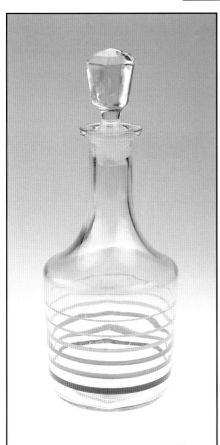

The #702 32 oz. decanter, $30-40.

This pattern was known as the Decoration #171 line produced in 1933. The catalogs did not list a pitcher in this pattern. Only the #102 decanter with ground stopper, $35-50, the #151 cocktail shaker with aluminum top, $50-75, and five sizes of tumblers were listed. Here are four #1241 1 ½ oz. 2" tumblers, $10-12 each.

The Pinch Line was listed in the Butler Brothers catalog and sold in a crystal decorated version. This was similar to the Decoration #171 listed in the Anchor Hocking catalogs, but the Butler Brothers catalog did list the pitcher.

The Fiesta Block decoration 80 oz. pitcher #790/4321 was produced in 1938, $40-50. It was sold with the #3519 9 ½ oz. 4 ¾" tall tumbler.

Left to right: #790 80 oz. jug Decoration #2145 produced from 1934 to 1938, $40-50; 9 ½ oz. tall tumbler #3519/2145, 4 ¼", $10-12; 9 oz. table tumbler #3501/2145, 4", $10-12; 6 oz. small hi-ball #3511/2145, 3 ½", $8-10.

Left to right: 6 oz. champagne, 4 7/8", $10-12; 6 ¾ oz. sherbet #333/2145, 3 ½", $10-12; sherbet plate #828/2145, 6", $10-12; 3 ½ oz. footed cocktail #182/2145, 3 3/8", $8-10.

Left to right: #790/2079 80 oz. pitcher with white spiral bands and blue top and bottom bands, $40-50; #790/2078 80 oz. pitcher with white spiral bands and red top and bottom bands, $40-50. Both pitchers were available with five sizes of glasses.

Left to right: #790/55 Rainbow Stripes decoration 80 oz. pitcher produced from 1938 to 1942, $50-60; #790/2672 Rainbow Hairlines decoration 80 oz. pitcher produced from 1938 to 1942, $50-60.

The Betsy Ross decoration was produced from 1938 to 1942. This set consists of one #790/1776 80 oz. pitcher, $60-75, and six #3321/1776 9 oz. 4 ¾" blown tumblers, $10-15 for each glass. There is also a 5 oz. tumbler in this design (not shown).

Rainbow Bands decoration 80 oz. jug #790/2665 produced from 1938 to 1942, $40-50; 11 oz. glass, 4 ¾", $10-12; 9 oz. glass, 3 ½", $8-10.

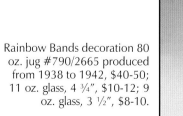

Left to right: Striped #790 80 oz. jug, $40-50; #790/5 Fiesta Stripe decoration 80 oz. jug made in the late 1940s, $40-50.

The #790/5 Fiesta Striped 80 oz. jug could be purchased in sets with maroon and white, tangerine and white, yellow and white, or green and white 11 oz. or 15 oz. glasses, $40-50 for the pitcher and $8-10 for each glass.

Another striped decoration on the #790 80 oz. jug, $40-50.

91

This version of the striped #790 80 oz. jug was sold with six 9 oz. 4 ¾" blown table tumblers #3321, $40-50 for the pitcher and $12-15 for each glass.

The #790 Banded decoration 80 oz. jug, $40-50, with six 11 oz. 4 ¾" glasses, $8-10 for each glass.

This is the Frosted and Colored Bands decoration produced from 1938 to 1942. The glasses were made in red, yellow, green, and blue bands. The #790/2670 80 oz. pitcher was supplied to go with the set (not shown).

Rare frosted color banded refreshment set, $200-250 for the set, $80-100 for the pitcher, $20-30 for each 15 oz. 6" ice tea glass.

This photo brings up an interesting point when trying to identify glassware. The pitcher in the middle is an Anchor Hocking #790 80 oz. jug. The pitchers to the left and right of the center pitcher have been located with Libbey marked glasses. I am not sure if these two pitchers are an intermediate Anchor Hocking design or a design produced by Libbey. Still, these two pitchers have all the characteristics of Anchor Hocking and not Libbey designs. I have not found anything like this pitcher in the Libbey literature. Any information about this design would be helpful.

The striped pitcher, $40-50, with three 8 oz. 3 ¾" glasses, $10-12 for each glass. This decoration was available with three different sizes of glasses.

Striped pitcher produced in the early 1930s, $40-50, with six #81 9 oz. 3" tumblers, $10-12 for each tumbler.

Several additional pieces of glass were produced in this pattern. Left to right: #68 12 oz. ice tea glass, 6", $12-15; #61 9 oz. tumbler, 3", $10-12; #63 5 oz. fruit juice, 3", $10-12; shot glass, 3", $10-12; #134 high sherbet, 5", $12-15.

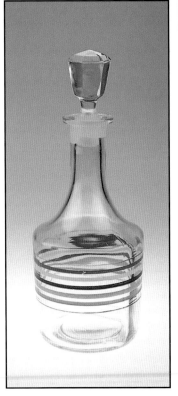

The #702 decanter with ground stopper, $50-60.

The striped pitcher was also sold with this intermediate design pitcher, $50-75, with six #81 9 oz. 3" tumblers, $10-12 for each tumbler.

The #700 80 oz. striped jug was produced during the early 1930s, $50-60.

The #380 Colored Line Decoration #28 80 oz. jug produced in the early 1930s, $50-60.

The #380 Colored Line 80 oz. jug produced in the early 1930s, $50-60, with six 11 oz. 4 ¾" glasses, $10-12 for each glass.

Another #380 Colored Line 80 oz. jug produced in the early 1930s, $50-60, with six 9 oz. 4" footed glasses, $15-20 for each glass.

Left to right: 9 oz. footed glass, 4", $15-20; 5 oz. glass, 3", $10-12; 2 ½ oz. glass, 1 ½", $10-12.

This pitcher shape was used for other well-known patterns such as Cameo. There are several fiesta striped versions of this pitcher, $35-45, with six 9 oz. 4 ½" glasses, $10-12 for each glass.

Striped #702 decanter with ground stopper, $50-60.

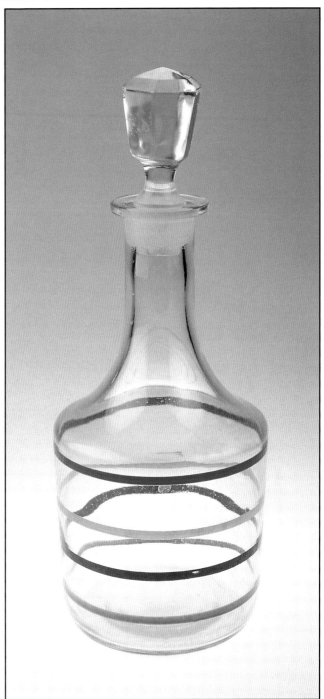

The Butler Brothers catalog did list the 4-colored banded decanter with another different pitcher design. Evidently, this design was used for many years.

Two more fiesta-striped pitchers, $35-45 for each pitcher.

Two more fiesta-striped pitchers, $35-45 for each pitcher. The pitcher on the right has the same fiesta striped pattern that was applied to two earlier pitcher designs and a myriad of accessory pieces.

Another fiesta-striped pitcher, $35-45.

CHAPTER NINE

Juice Pitchers

The Strawberry decoration was produced in 1950, $75-100 for the entire set, $35-50 for the #187/353 80 oz. pitcher, $10-12 for each #65/353 11 oz. 4 ¾" tumbler.

Left to right: #187/353 80 oz. pitcher (1950), $35-50; #146/353 36 oz. pitcher (1950), $25-35.

The Forget-Me-Not decoration was produced in 1950. Left to right: #187/356 80 oz. pitcher, $35-50; #146/356 36 oz. pitcher, $25-35; #116/356 11 oz. tumbler, 4 ¾", $10-12; #113/356 6 oz. fruit juice, 3", $12-15.

Left to right: #146/347 36 oz. pitcher (1950 to 1952), $20-25; crystal 36 oz. pitcher, $25-30; #146/814 Tomatoes decoration 36 oz. pitcher (1951 to 1952), $20-25.

The #100/9 7-Piece Fruit Juice Set with the #113/347 6 oz. glasses, $40-50 for the entire set, $20-25 for the pitcher, $2-5 for each glass.

The #100/10 Tomato decoration 7-Piece Fruit Juice Set with the #113/377 6 oz. 3 5/8" glasses, $40-50 for the entire set, $20-25 for the pitcher, $2-5 for each glass.

Left to right: #187/809 Tulip decoration 80 oz. pitcher (1951 to 1952), $40-50; #187/361 Daisy decoration 80 oz. pitcher (1950), $40-50.

The #400/120 7-Piece Tomato Fruit Juice Set, $60-75 for the entire set, $20-25 for the box.

The #100/7 Large Flower and Leaves decoration 7-Piece Fruit Juice Set (1950 to 1951), $80-100 for the entire set, $40-50 for the pitcher, $10-12 for each #116/350 11 oz. 4 ½" tumbler.

The Large Flower and Leaves decoration sets were furnished with three sizes of glasses. Left to right: #118/350 15 oz. iced tea glass, 5", $12-15; #116/350 11 oz. tumbler, 4 ½", $10-12; #113/350 6 oz. fruit juice, 3", $8-10.

The #100/13 Large Flower decoration 7-Piece Fruit Juice Set (1950), $80-100 for the entire set, $40-50 for the #187/359 80 oz. pitcher, $10-12 for each #65/359 11 oz. 4 ½" tumbler.

The #187/587 Modern Floral decoration 80 oz. pitcher (1950 to 1951), $40-50, with four #3526/587 15 oz. 6 ¼", long boy iced tea glasses, $10-12 for each glass. The glasses for this decoration came in three colors and five sizes; however, not all the colors were made in each size. The pitchers were listed in the catalogs with only red flowers.

Left to right: the #187/587 Modern Floral decoration 80 oz. pitcher, $40-50; #146/587 Modern Floral decoration 36 oz. pitcher, $35-45.

Left to right: #187/357 Tulip decoration 80 oz. pitcher (1950 to 1951), $40-50; #118/357 15 oz. iced tea glass, 5", $10-12.

Left to right: #187/348 Ship decoration 80 oz. pitcher (1950 to 1951), $40-50; #187/608 Ship decoration 80 oz. pitcher (1951 to 1952), $40-50. The pitchers are basically the same design with the exception of the waves under the sailboat.

Two different versions of the #187/348 Ship decoration 80 oz. pitcher, $40-50 for each version. Notice the sailboats lean a different direction on each pitcher and both pitchers have the same wave design.

The #100/3 Ship decoration 7-Piece Refreshment Set, $100-125 for the entire set, $40-50 for the pitcher, $12-15 for each #116/348 11 oz. 4 ½" glass.

Carrier with six #116/348 11 oz. 4 ½" glasses, $60-75, $15-20 for the carrier only.

The Wild Flower decoration #187/553 80 oz. pitcher (1951 to 1952), $40-50, with four #475/553 11 oz. 4 ½" tapered tumblers, $10-12 for each tumbler. The pitcher was listed with only the red flowers, but the glasses were listed with red, yellow, and blue flowers. Only the red flowered glasses had more than one size. The red flowered glass came in a 5 oz. fruit juice, 11 oz. tumbler, and 15 oz. iced tea.

Left to right: the #187/553 Wild Flower decoration 80 oz. pitcher, $40-50; #146/553 Wild Flower decoration 36 oz. pitcher, $35-45.

The Phlox decoration #187/599 80 oz. pitcher (1951 to 1952), $40-50, with six #475/599 11 oz. 4 ½" tapered tumblers, $10-12 for each tumbler.

Two additional Fiesta Striped 80 oz. pitchers,
$40-50 for each pitcher.

Envelope containing one of the
monthly Butler Brothers special
bulletins.

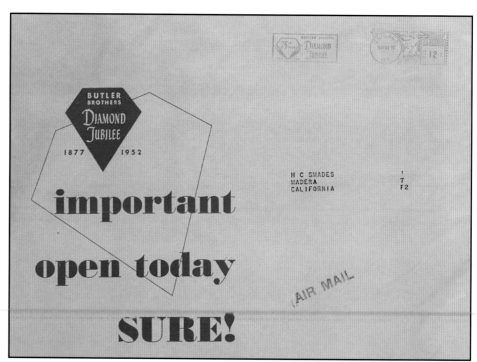

108

Letter that accompanied the special bulletin.

The first page of the monthly special bulletin listed an Anchor Hocking juice pitcher.

Inside the monthly bulletin you will notice the Fiesta Striped juice pitcher listed for only $3.75 a dozen.

The Fiesta Bands decoration #187/39 80 oz. pitcher (1951 to 1952), $40-50, with six #65/69 11 oz. 4 ½" tumblers, $10-12 for each tumbler.

Left to right: #187/360 Rose decoration 80 oz. pitcher (1950), $40-50; Roly Poly 9 oz. glass, 4", $8-10.

Left to right: #146/360 Rose decoration 36 oz. pitcher (1950), $40-50; Roly Poly 5 oz. fruit juice glass, 3 ¼", $8-10.

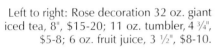

Left to right: Rose decoration 32 oz. giant iced tea, 8", $15-20; 11 oz. tumbler, 4 ¾", $5-8; 6 oz. fruit juice, 3 ½", $8-10.

Another floral decoration on the 80 oz. pitcher, $40-50, with six 11 oz. 4 ½" tapered glasses, $10-12 for each glass.

The Square Dance Party Set, $60-75 for the 80 oz. pitcher, $10-15 for each 11 oz. 4 ½" tumbler. The set would include the Hoe Down, Partners All (not shown), Swing Her High, and Do Si Do tumblers.

The Modern Flower decoration #187/803 80 oz. pitcher (1950 to 1951), $40-50, with four #65/805 11 oz. 4 ½" tumblers, $10-12 for each tumbler.

The Daisy decoration #187/815 80 oz. pitcher (1951 to 1952), $40-50, with six #475/815 11 oz. 4 ½" tapered glasses, $10-12 for each glass.

The #400/116 7-Piece Set Daisy decoration #400/116 in the original box, $15-20 for the box only.

The Spring Flowers decoration #187/562 80 oz. pitcher (1951 to 1952), $40-50. This pattern also includes a 36 oz. pitcher and six sizes of glasses. Only the 6 ½" long boy iced tea glass was produced in colors other than red. This glass was made in red, yellow, and light green colors.

Frosted 80 oz. pitcher, $60-75, with six 11 oz. 4 ¾" glasses, $15-20 for each glass.

Frosted 36 oz. pitcher, $50-60, with six 5 oz. 3" Roly Poly glasses, $12-15 for each glass.

Frosted 36 oz. pitcher, $50-60, with six 5 oz. 3" glasses, $12-15 for each glass.

Frosted 36 oz. pitcher with hand-painted flowers, $60-75.

Frosted 36 oz. pitcher with hand-painted flowers, $60-75 for the pitcher, $10-12 for the 6 oz. 3 ½" glass.

Frosted 36 oz. pitcher with hand-painted flowers, $60-75 for the pitcher, $10-12 for the 6 oz. 3 ½" glass.

Frosted 36 oz. pitcher, $50-60, with six 5 oz. 3" glasses, $12-15 for each glass.

Frosted 36 oz. pitcher, $60-75, with six 5 oz. 3" glasses, $12-15 for each glass.

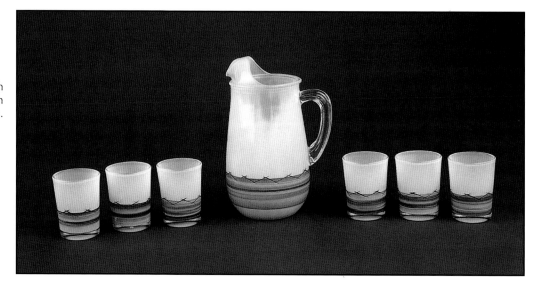

Frosted 36 oz. pitcher, $60-75, with two 5 oz. 3" glasses, $12-15 for each glass.

Frosted 36 oz. pitcher, $50-60.

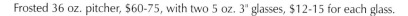

CHAPTER TEN
Etched Patterns

Anchor Hocking probably produced more than twenty different etched patterns over the years. Many of the patterns have been produced for over twenty years. I have attempted to show some of the major patterns, but realize there are numerous other patterns that exist.

There are two basic methods for applying etched designs on glass. The first method employs hydrofluoric acid. The item to be etched is first coated with paraffin wax. Then the wax is removed in the areas where the company wanted the design. The glass was then subjected to a hydrofluoric acid mist. The acid literally dissolves the glass in all areas not protected by the wax. Once the design is etched into the glass, the wax is removed. Acid etched designs have a very uniform frosted appearance. In the second method, the glass is literally etched by grinding.

Artisans use a spinning wheel coated with diamond dust to remove some of the glass. If you closely examine designs produced by this method, you will see a series of parallel lines in the etched areas. The lines were made by the particles of diamond dust scraping across the glass surface.

When first collecting glass, it is also very confusing to distinguish etched and pressed glass designs. When a design is etched into glass using a spinning wheel coated with diamond dust, the edges in the design are very sharp and well pronounced. If the glass design was pressed in a mold, the edges in the design are rounded and smooth. Both of these types of glass have a very distinct and different "feel" to the touch.

This is a close-up of the etching done with a diamond wheel. You will notice that there are very sharply defined parallel lines in the etching.

Assorted glasses with the Laurel Cut (Cut #411), $1-3 for each glass.

Assorted glasses with the Laurel Cut, $1-3 for each glass.

The Roly Poly glass was used to sell jelly and the label stated, "Genuine American Cut Glass".

Assorted glasses with the Coin Dot Cut, $1-3 for each glass.

Assorted glasses with the Laurel and Bands Cut (Cut #401), $1-3 for each glass.

Mixer with the Laurel and Bands Cut, $40-50.

Assorted glasses with the Coins and Bands Cut (Cut #120), $1-3 for each glass.

Roly Poly glass with Grape Cut (Cut #210), $2-3.

Berwick glasses with Grape Cut, $2-3 for each glass.

Norst Cut glasses, $1-2 for each glass.

Rose Cut Early American glasses, $3-5 for each glass.

Miscellaneous etched pieces made at Hillyard's Gift Shop in Bremen, Ohio.

Etched glass made for people in the Order of the Eastern Star. Prices for these pieces would depend on the sentimental value for the collector. The three pieces of glass are surrounded by a shoulder decoration worn by officers of the Order.

Large apothecary Jar with the etching dedicated to Ruby Moore, $30-40.

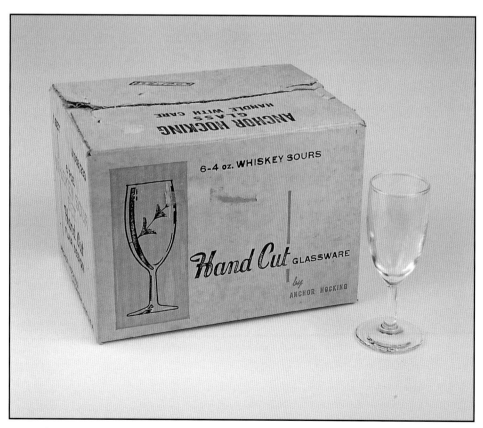

Set of six 4 oz. whiskey glasses, 5 ½", $30-40 for the set, $3-4 for each glass, $10-15 for the box and $5-10 for the insert card from the artisan.

Our Congratulations:

You are now the owner of a set of "Bremen Crystal" hand cut glassware - the finest product of Anchor Hocking Glass.

Each piece of glass has been artistically hand cut by American craftsmen - artisans who in many cases have practiced the art for over twenty-five years. The touch of the artist is apparent in each piece of glass (proof of this hand craftsmanship is evidenced by the slight variance in design from glass to glass.)

Cut glassware should be cared for with the same care given any fine crystal-with no fear of the decoration ever washing or wearing off.

We wish you years of pleasant service.

Your artisan _M Fox_

Bremen Crystal
A product of Anchor Hocking Glass
Lancaster, Ohio U.S.A.

Each set of glasses had a card included in the box that was signed by the artisan who etched the glasses.

Finely etched brandy snifter and wine glass, $10-15 for each piece. These items were probably etched in Bremen, Ohio.

Boxed set of etched glasses made in Bremen, Ohio, $40-50 for the complete set of eight 5 oz. juice glasses, $10-15 for the box only.

123

Top left: Etched sherbet with frosted base, 3 ¼", $15-20.

Bottom left: Etched champagne glasses with pastel frosted bases, 4 ¾", $15-20 for each glass.

Top right: Etched 32 oz. decanter, $30-40.

CHAPTER ELEVEN

Miscellaneous Glasses

Honey Gold Berwick glasses, $5-8 for each size of glass.

Gold Band and Hairline decoration applied to
Berwick glasses, $5-8 for each size of glass.

Extremely rare fired-on pastel colored #3321 9 oz. blown tumblers, 4 5/8", $30-40 for each glass.

There is some confusion between Anchor Hocking and Federal glasses. While the basic shape is the same for all the glasses in the photograph, you will notice that the fourth and seventh glasses from the left do not have the three ridges circling the center of the glass. These without the ridges are Federal glasses. Anchor Hocking made all the remaining glasses shown. Anchor Hocking made five sizes of this style of glass, but Federal only listed one size in the catalogs.

Unidentified glass with the "anchor over H" emblem in the bottom of the glass, $5-0.

The Venetian tumblers were made from 1949 to 1950. The pattern was available in both plain and decorated versions. The decorated versions were either alternating light and dark blue lines or colored lines (orange, yellow, green, and orange in that order from the top of the glass). Left to right: 14 oz. iced tea #3108, 4 ½", $5-8; 9 ½ oz. tumbler #3106, 3 ½", $5-8; 5 oz. fruit juice #3103, 3", $5-8; 5 oz. fruit juice #3103/293, 3", $8-10.

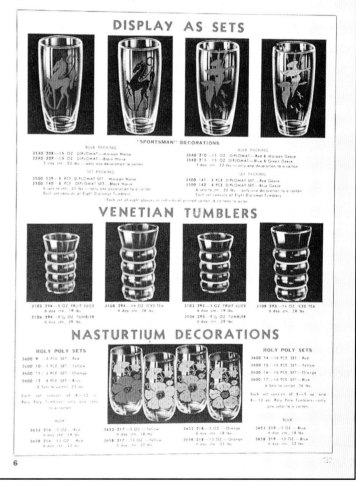

The Venetian tumblers were listed in the 1949 Anchor Hocking catalog.

Two unidentified glasses with the "anchor over H" emblem in the bottom of the glass, $5-8 for each glass.